THE KETO BREADS COOKBOOK

Delicious Recipes for Baking Low-Carb Bread, Buns, Muffins & Cookies to Maximize your Weight Loss

Kaitlyn Donnelly

DISCLAIMER

The recipes and information in this book are provided for educational purposes only. Please always consult a licensed professional before making changes to your lifestyle or diet. The author and publisher shall have neither liability nor responsibility to anyone with respect to any loss or damage caused or alleged to be caused directly or indirectly by the information contained in this book. All trademarks and brands within this book are for clarifying purposes only and are owned by the owners themselves, not affiliated with this document.

Images from shutterstock.com

CONTENTS

INTRODUCTION

Man shall not live on bread alone that is why this book, although called Keto Bread, is also full of muffin, pizza and cookie recipes. Diet is not a judgment, remember? And bread is, for many people not just a slice of dough but also a tradition kept for centuries. So why not adapt these traditions to Keto and enjoy food diversity? This book will introduce many national recipes of Indian, Armenian, and Jewish cuisines. It will present a number of muffins from unflavored to sweet, and cookie ideas.

One of Keto's tasks is to reprogram our metabolism in such way that it takes energy from glucose, not from fats. Just a quick reminder of how the carbohydrates "function" in the body. carbs get broken down into glucose which insulin then takes throughout the body to be used as energy. This is a very easy and fast process for the body to do, which is why this is the first choice the body makes for energy. All parts of the body can use glucose for energy. If we consume too much glucose, our bodies will then create little packets of glucose called glycogen. But we can only store limited amounts of glycogen, so any excess glucose beyond what we can store is converted into fat.

We are interested in consuming foods that are high in fiber and low in overall carbs.

GUIDE TO LOW CARB FLOURS

ALMOND FLOUR

Almond flour is perhaps one of the most popular low carb flours. Almond flour is made from blanched almonds. It is finely ground and doesn't contain almond skin. The flour is rich in vitamins and minerals and provides the most calcium compared to any other nut.

One cup of almond flour contains 168 calories, 13.3 g fat, 6 g carbohydrates, 6 g protein and 3 g dietary fiber.

Since almond flour can go bad fast, it is recommended to store it in the fridge or freezer after opening.

ALMOND MEAL

Almond meal is not the same as almond flour. Rather than blanching the almonds to remove the skins, the skin of the almonds is kept on. It has a bit coarser texture than almond flour but still bakes the same. If you are running low on almond meal you can grind almonds using a blender or food processor.

One cup or 100 g of almond meal contains 607 calories, 48.2 g fat, 21.8 g carbohydrates, 21.8 g protein and 10.7 g dietary fiber.

COCONUT FLOUR

Coconut flour is higher in carbs, but also high in fiber and protein. One cup of coconut flour contains 360 calories, 16 g fat, 88 g carbohydrates, 32 g protein and 64 g dietary fiber.

Coconut flour absorbs a lot of liquid and tends to need a lot more moisture when baking. Do not skimp on the eggs, butter or extra moisture in recipes. It's OK to use 2–3 eggs per ¼ cup coconut flour. Also when cooking with coconut flour allow the batter to stand and thicken for a while.

Keep the flour in an airtight sealed bag or container in a cool, dark place.

FLAX MEAL

Flax meal is ground flax seeds or linseeds—the seeds of the plant which is used to make linen cloth. The whole seeds need to be ground into meal to get their full nutritional benefit. Flax seeds are a good source of vitamin B1, Copper and Omega-3. One cup or 165 g of flax meal contains 770 calories, 55 g fat, 55 g carbohydrates, 33 g protein and 44 g dietary fiber.

What's great about baking with flax meal is that not only can it replace flour in recipes, but it can also replace eggs. Eggs help bind the ingredients; so does the flax. To replace one egg, mix one tablespoon ground flax meal with three tablespoons of water and allow it to swell.

It is best to store flax meal in the fridge before and after opening.

PUMPKIN SEED MEAL

Pumpkin seed meal is made by processing raw or toasted pumpkin seeds into a thick meal. One cup of pumpkin seeds contains 160 calories, 12 g fat, 4 g carbohydrates, 9 g protein and 1 g dietary fiber. Pumpkin seed meal can also be a healthy, delicious substitute for bread crumbs, or used for sprinkling in all possible recipes.

PSYLLIUM HUSK

Although psyllium husk is not flour, it is used as a thickener to help the ingredients bind together. Psyllium husk forms a gel that is stable only up to temperatures of about 176°F (80°C), depending on the amount used in the recipe.

One tablespoon of psyllium has 53 calories, 0 g fat, 15 g carbohydrates, 0 g protein and 13.5 g dietary fiber.

In stores psyllium husk is often sold as COLON CLEANSER.

TO SIFT OR NOT TO SIFT

Sifting is a process that filters out any lumps in the flour and aerates it at the same time. Sifted flour is much lighter than unsifted flour. It's enriched with oxygen and is easier to mix into other ingredients when forming a cake batter or making dough. Under the load of its own weight any flour becomes compressed and heavy. After sifting it gains consistency and is more likely to be measured with exact accuracy. My answer is yes, do sift your flour if possible.

GUIDE TO LOW CARB SWEETENERS USED IN BAKING

STEVIA

Stevia is a herb, which is commonly known as "sugar leaf". Stevia belongs to a group of non-nutritive sweeteners. This means it has no calories, vitamins or any other nutrients. Stevia may come in powder, drops or glycerite. It is better to opt for liquid stevia, because some brands additionally mix in artificial sweeteners. Some of these may be hidden carbs you don't need, or they may raise blood sugar.

ERYTHRITOL

Erythritol is a sugar alcohol that is made through fermentation. Even though sugar alcohols are technically carbohydrates, we do not completely absorb them, most of them do not raise blood sugar levels and therefore don't count as "net" carbs. Erythritol is 60 to 80 percent as sweet as sugar so you may need to use a bit more than sugar.

XYLITOL

Xylitol is a sugar alcohol that can be processed from trees like birch, but it can also be made with an industrial process that transforms a plant fiber called xylan into xylitol. Like stevia, xylitol doesn't contain any vitamins, minerals or protein.

NB! Xylitol can be toxic to dogs, so keep it safely out of their reach!

SORBITOL

Sorbitol is another sugar alcohol that is manufactured from cornstarch. As it can withstand high temperatures it can be used in baking. It also often comes in powder form.

SUGAR ALCOHOLS GLYCEMIC INDEX

Sugar Alcohols	GI (glucose = 100)	Calories / 100g	Net Carbs / 100g
Maltitol	36	270	67
Xylitol	13	300	75
Isomalt	9	210	52
Sorbitol	9	250	62
Lactitol	6	300	75
Erythritol	0	20	5
Mannitol	0	150	37

Studies show that our body can only partially derive calories and carbs from sugar alcohols. The exact amount depends on the type of sugar alcohols.

Some sugar alcohols such as Xylitol and Mannitol are known for their laxative effects when recommended intake is exceeded.

Be aware: In many cases, net carbs from Maltitol that is commonly used in "low-carb" products, are not added to the total net carbs count!

The best sweetener from sugar alcohols with minimum negative effects is Erythritol (lowest in calories and net carbs and has no effect on blood sugar).

COCONUT SUGAR

Coconut sugar is a natural sugar made from sugary circulating fluid of the coconut plant. Coconut Sugar has a GI of 35, which puts it in the low range. This is much lower than table sugar, which is somewhere around 60 but higher than some other sugar substitutes. It has 4 g carbohydrates and 15 calories per teaspoon.

Overview of Sweeteners (average estimated nutrition values)

Use mostly	Stevia	Erythritol	Monk fruit powder	
Glycemic Index	0	0	0	The exact amount of net carbs varies for all products. Most products also contain other sweeteners such as inulin, so keep that in mind, as the nutrition values and net carbs vary for different products!
Net Carbs / 100g	5	5	0 - 25	
Net Carbs in grams / serving	0 (few drops)	0.5 (tbsp)	0 (pinch)	
Kcal / 100g	20	20	0 - 100	

Use in moderation	Mannitol	Tagatose	Inulin-based sweeteners	Xylitol	Yacon syrup / powder
Glycemic Index	0	3	0	13	1
Net Carbs / 100g	37	37	25 - 37	60	40 / 62
Net Carbs in grams / serving	3.7 (tbsp)	3.7 (tbsp)	2.5 - 3.7 (tbsp)	6.2 (tbsp)	8 / 6.2 (tbsp)
Kcal / 100g	150	150	100 - 150	240	168 / 250

Other to be used in moderation: lucuma powder, freeze-dried berry powder, dark chocolate (75% and more)

Use sparingly	Raw honey	Coconut palm sugar	Maple syrup	Date syrup	Blackstrap molasses
Glycemic Index	32 - 85	35	54	40 - 50	55
Net Carbs / 100g	82	92	67	64	61
Net Carbs in grams / serving	17.3 (tbsp)	11 (tbsp)	13.4 (tbsp)	13.4 (tbsp)	12.1 (tbsp)
Kcal / 100g	304	370	260	284	235

Other to be used sparingly: dried dates and figs, fresh fruit juices

Avoid Completely: HFCS and sugar, agave syrup, artificial sweeteners (Splenda, Equal, aspartame, etc.)

CLOUD BREAD

SERVINGS: 8 | PREP TIME: 15 min. | COOK TIME: 20 min.

CARBS: 0 g | FAT: 10 g | PROTEIN: 7 g | CALORIES: 122

INGREDIENTS

- *3 Tbsp cream cheese, room temperature*
- *3 eggs, separated*
- *½ tsp baking powder*
- *Salt to taste*

DIRECTIONS

1. Whip to combine the egg yolks, the cream cheese and salt.
2. In a separate bowl whip the egg yolks and baking powder.
3. Stir 2 mixtures together until combined.
4. Preheat the oven to 300°F.
5. Line a baking sheet with parchment paper and spoon the bread mixture onto it leaving some space in between.
6. Cook for 15–20 minutes.

FLAX SEED BREAD

SERVINGS: 8 | PREP TIME: 15 min. | COOK TIME: 1 hour.

CARBS: 9 g | FAT: 13 g | PROTEIN: 6 g | CALORIES: 167

INGREDIENTS

- *1¼ cup flax seed, finely ground*
- *1 cup water*
- *Salt to taste*
- *Coconut oil for greasing*

DIRECTIONS

1. Preheat the oven to 450°F.
2. Grease a metal baking dish with cooking spray or coconut oil.
3. In a bowl mix salt with ground flaxseed. Add water and stir fast.
4. While stirring the flaxseed absorbs water and becomes a sticky mass.
5. Shape the mass into a ball and place it into a greased metal dish.
6. Place into the oven for 1 hour.

COTTAGE BREAD

SERVINGS: 6 | PREP TIME: 15 min. | COOK TIME: 45 min.

CARBS: 6 g | FAT: 6.3 g | PROTEIN: 8.4 g | CALORIES: 109

INGREDIENTS

- *7–8 oz cottage cheese*
- *1 egg*
- *1 tsp flax seed, ground*
- *1 tsp sesame seeds, ground*
- *3 Tbsp oat bran*
- *2 Tbsp wheat bran*
- *½ tsp baking powder*
- *1½–2 oz sunflower seeds*
- *Salt to taste*
- *Turmeric powder to taste*

DIRECTIONS

1. In a medium-sized bowl combine cottage cheese, egg, flax seed and sesame seeds.
2. Add salt and turmeric powder if used.
3. Add brans and seeds and give a good stir.
4. Let stand for 10 minutes
5. Preheat the oven to 428°F.
6. Line a baking dish with parchment paper and with wet hands shape the cottage cheese mixture into a ball and bake in the oven for 45 minutes.

SPRING ONION BREAD

SERVINGS: 6 | PREP TIME: 15 min. | COOK TIME: 20 min.

CARBS: 0.5 g | FAT: 1.8 g | PROTEIN: 2.2 g | CALORIES: 27

INGREDIENTS

- *3 Tbsp cream cheese, room temperature*
- *3 eggs, separated*
- *1 Tbsp apple vinegar*
- *3 Tbsp spring onions, minced*
- *Salt to taste*

DIRECTIONS

1. Whip to combine the egg yolks, the cream cheese, and spring onions.
2. In a separate bowl whip the egg whites with apple vinegar and salt.
3. In batches start adding egg whites mixture into the egg yolks mixture.
4. Preheat the oven to 300°F.
5. Line a baking sheet with parchment paper and spoon the bread mixture onto it making sure the spoonfuls are separated.
6. Cook for 20 minutes.

FLATBREAD

SERVINGS: 6 | PREP TIME: 20 min. | COOK TIME: 20 min.

CARBS: 2 g | FAT: 6.6 g | PROTEIN: 2 g | CALORIES: 70

INGREDIENTS

- *1 Tbsp butter*
- *8 Tbsp almond flour, sifted*
- *Salt to taste*
- *1 cup water*

DIRECTIONS

1. Combine the sifted flour with salt and butter.
2. Add water and knead the dough.
3. Let stand for 15 minutes.
4. Preheat the oven to 350°F.
5. Line a baking sheet with parchment paper and flatten the dough into several flatbreads.
6. Bake for 15 minutes, then flip over and bake for 5 minutes on the other side.

CHEESE FLATBREAD

SERVINGS: 6 | PREP TIME: 20 min. | COOK TIME: 20 min.

CARBS: 5 g | FAT: 11.3 g | PROTEIN: 12.3 g | CALORIES: 170

INGREDIENTS

- *1 cup buttermilk, warm*
- *2 cups almond flour, sifted*
- *5½ oz hard cheese, grated*
- *½ tsp baking powder*
- *Salt to taste*

DIRECTIONS

1. Add salt and baking powder to buttermilk.
2. Combine the grated cheese with flour and add to buttermilk.
3. Knead the dough and shape it into 5 balls.
4. Preheat the oven to 350°F.
5. Line a baking sheet with parchment paper and flatten the balls into 5 flatbreads.
6. Bake for 15 minutes, then flip over and bake for 5 minutes on the other side.

MATZO BREAD

SERVINGS: 6 | PREP TIME: 15 min. | COOK TIME: 4 min.

CARBS: 1 g | FAT: 2.2 g | PROTEIN: 1 g | CALORIES: 28

INGREDIENTS

- *1 cup almond flour, sifted*
- *½ cup water*
- *Salt to taste*

DIRECTIONS

1. Preheat the oven to 475°F.
2. Add flour into a mixing bowl and add the water 1 Tbsp at a time stirring. Add salt.
3. Knead the dough and divide into 4 balls.
4. Line the baking sheet with parchment paper. Roll the dough into balls. Flatten the balls into 5 thin round disks
5. Using a fork, pierce each round all over, to prevent rising.
6. Bake for 2 minutes on each side.

PITA BREAD

SERVINGS: 8 | PREP TIME: 20 min. | COOK TIME: 15 min.

CARBS: 1.6 g | FAT: 6.9 g | PROTEIN: 1.6 g | CALORIES: 73

INGREDIENTS

- *2 cups almond flour, sifted*
- *½ cup water*
- *2 Tbsp olive oil*
- *Salt to taste*
- *1 tsp black cumin*

DIRECTIONS

1. Preheat the oven to 400°F.
2. Combine flour with salt. Add the water and olive oil.
3. Knead the dough and let stand for 15 minutes
4. Shape the dough into 8 balls.
5. Line a baking sheet with parchment paper and flatten the balls into 8 thin rounds.
6. Sprinkle with black cumin.
7. Bake for 15 minutes

INDIAN PURI BREAD

SERVINGS: 6 | PREP TIME: 20 min. | COOK TIME: 1 min.

CARBS: 16 g | FAT: 3 g | PROTEIN: 3 g | CALORIES: 106

INGREDIENTS

- *1 cup almond flour, sifted*
- *½ cup warm water*
- *2 Tbsp clarified butter*
- *1 cup olive oil for frying*
- *Salt to taste*

DIRECTIONS

1. Salt the water and add the flour.
2. Make a hole in the center of the dough and pour in warm clarified butter.
3. Knead the dough and let stand for 15 minutes, covered.
4. Shape into 6 balls.
5. Flatten the balls into 6 thin rounds using a rolling pin or your hands
6. Heat enough oil to completely cover a round in a frying pan and, when hot, place a puri in it.
7. Fry for 20 seconds on each side.
8. Place on a paper towel. Repeat with the rest of the puri.

SEMOLINA FLATBREAD

SERVINGS: 6 | PREP TIME: 1 hour 10 min. | COOK TIME: 30 min.

CARBS: 61 g | FAT: 18 g | PROTEIN: 11 g | CALORIES: 456

INGREDIENTS

- 18 oz semolina
- 2 tsp instant yeast
- 1 cup warm water
- ½ cup olive oil
- Small bunch spring onions, chopped
- Salt to taste
- 1 egg yolk for brushing
- Sesame seeds for sprinkling

DIRECTIONS

1. Mix semolina, yeast and salt.
2. Pour in warm water and knead the dough.
3. Let rise for 1 hour.
4. Knead the dough, adding the chopped spring onions. Shape into several balls.
5. Line a baking sheet with parchment paper and flatten the balls into thin rounds with a rolling pin.
6. Brush with egg yolk and sprinkle with sesame seeds.
7. Bake for at 464 F for 10 min then reduce to 392F and bake for 20 min.

FOCACCIA

SERVINGS: 8 | PREP TIME: 15 min. | COOK TIME: 25 min.

CARBS: 3.4 g | FAT: 19 g | PROTEIN: 10.2 g | CALORIES: 245

INGREDIENTS

- *1 cup almond flour*
- *1 cup flaxseed, ground*
- *6 eggs*
- *¼ cup olive oil*
- *1 tsp baking powder*
- *2 garlic cloves, minced*
- *1 tsp dried basil*
- *1 tsp dried oregano*
- *Salt to taste*

DIRECTIONS

1. Preheat the oven to 350°F.
2. Combine flour, flaxseed and the spices in a mixing bowl. Add baking powder and give a good stir to all dry ingredients.
3. Add the garlic and the eggs, one by one, whisking to combine.
4. Add olive oil, whisk.
5. Line a baking pan with parchment paper and pour in the batter.
6. Bake for 25 minutes.

LAHMAJOUN (ARMENIAN PIZZA)

SERVINGS: 6 | PREP TIME: 1 hour 15 min. | COOK TIME: 10 min.

CARBS: 9.5 g | FAT: 28.3 g | PROTEIN: 20 g | CALORIES: 385

INGREDIENTS

- *1 cup almond flour*
- *3 Tbsp olive oil*
- *1 tsp instant yeast*
- *½ cup water*
- *Salt to taste*

For filling:

- *½ lb ground beef*
- *1 bell pepper, chopped*
- *1 tomato, chopped*
- *1 onion, chopped*
- *2 Tbsp tomato paste*
- *1 chili pepper, seeded*
- *2 Tbsp olive oil*
- *Bunch of dill and parsley, chopped*
- *Salt and pepper to taste*
- *Fresh greens for serving*

DIRECTIONS

1. Prepare the dough: add flour to a mixing bowl and make a hole in the middle. Add yeast and half of the water. Stir lightly and let stand for 15 minutes for yeast to activate.
2. Add the remaining water, olive oil, salt. Knead the dough and let stand for 1 hour.
3. In a blender mix the vegetables, dill and parsley and spices. Add tomato paste and olive oil, mix well.
4. Season the ground meat with salt and pepper and add to the blended vegetables. Blend again.
5. Shape the dough into several balls and roll out into thin rounds with a rolling pin.
6. Line a baking sheet with parchment paper and place the flat rounds onto it. Add 1–2 Tbsp of the filling and spread it all over the flatbread.
7. Bake for 5–10 minutes at 446°F.
8. Serve with fresh greens.

HERBY FLATBREAD

SERVINGS: 8 | PREP TIME: 20 min. | COOK TIME: 4 min.

CARBS: 48 g | FAT: 8 g | PROTEIN: 9.2 g | CALORIES: 303

INGREDIENTS

- *1 cup gram flour*
- *1½ Tbsp. olive oil*
- *Salt to taste*
- *¼ cup water*

For filling:
- *¼ cup gram flour*
- *1 tsp olive oil*
- *1 cup brown sugar*
- *1 Tbsp poppy seeds*
- *¼ tsp cardamom*
- *¼ tsp nutmeg*
- *2 Tbsp unsalted butter, melted for serving*

DIRECTIONS

1. Combine 1 cup gram flour, salt and 1 Tbsp olive oil. Add enough water to knead into a smooth dough. Knead with hands until soft.
2. Let stand for 10 minutes covered.
3. Add ½ Tbsp. olive oil and knead with hands.
4. Shape into an even number of balls (size of an apple) and put aside.
5. Heat 1 tsp olive oil in a frying pan and add ¼ cup gram flour. Cook, constantly stirring, until golden.
6. Transfer the cooked flour to a mixing bowl and combine with brown sugar, poppy seeds, cardamom and nutmeg.
7. Preheat the oven to 284°F.
8. Roll out the balls into flat rounds using a rolling pin. Place one rolled piece on a baking sheet. Add 1 Tbsp of the poppy seed mixture and cover with another rolled piece.
9. In a hot frying pan cook the breads for about 2 minutes on each side.
10. Brush with melted butter while hot.

OATMEAL TORTILLA

SERVINGS: 6 | PREP TIME: 15 min. | COOK TIME: 8 min.

CARBS: 3.5 g | FAT: 1 g | PROTEIN: 0.7 g | CALORIES: 26

INGREDIENTS

- *1 cup oatmeal*
- *⅓ cup hot water*
- *Salt to taste*
- *1 tsp salted butter, melted*

DIRECTIONS

1. Combine the oatmeal with salt.
2. Add melted butter to the hot water.
3. Knead the dough after adding the buttered water to the oatmeal. Add more water if needed.
4. Shape into two balls and roll into two rounds with a rolling pin.
5. Using a sharp knife cut each round into quarters and place in a hot frying pan.
6. Cook over medium for 3–5 minutes on each side.

SANGAK (IRANIAN FLATBREAD)

SERVINGS: 6 | PREP TIME: 3 hours 15 min. | COOK TIME: 6 min.

CARBS: 3.5 g | FAT: 1 g | PROTEIN: 0.7 g | CALORIES: 26

INGREDIENTS

- *4 cups almond flour*
- *2 ½ cups warm water*
- *1 Tbsp instant yeast*
- *12 tsp sesame seeds*
- *Salt to taste*

DIRECTIONS

1. Add 1 Tbsp of yeast to ½ cup warm water in a large bowl and let stand for 5 minutes to activate.
2. Add salt and 1 cup of water. Let stand for 10 minutes longer.
3. Add flour 1 cup at a time, and then add the remaining water.
4. Knead the dough and then shape into a ball and let stand for 3 hours covered.
5. Preheat the oven to 482°F.
6. With a rolling pin roll out the dough and divide into 6 balls. Roll each ball into ½ inch thick rounds.
7. Line a baking sheet with parchment paper and place the rolled rounds on it. With a finger make a small hole in the middle and add 2 tsp sesame seeds in each hole.
8. Bake for 3–4 minutes and then flip over and bake for 2 more minutes.

ITALIAN SEASONING BREAD

SERVINGS: 8 | PREP TIME: 15 min. | COOK TIME: 40 min.

CARBS: 2 g | FAT: 20 g | PROTEIN: 7 g | CALORIES: 26

INGREDIENTS

- *6 eggs*
- *½ cup coconut flour*
- *½ cup coconut oil, melted*
- *¼ tsp baking soda*
- *1 Tbsp flax seed*
- *½–1 tsp Italian seasoning*
- *Salt to taste*

DIRECTIONS

1. Combine eggs with coconut oil.
2. Add flour, Italian seasoning, soda and salt. Mix well until smooth.
3. Let the dough stand for 5–10 min then shape the bread or buns.
4. Line the baking sheet with parchment paper and place the bread on it. Sprinkle with flax seeds.
5. Bake at 356°F for 30–40 minutes.

SEED BREAD

SERVINGS: 8 | PREP TIME: 2 hours. | COOK TIME: 1 hour.

CARBS: 19 g | FAT: 10 g | PROTEIN: 8.2 g | CALORIES: 196

INGREDIENTS

- 1½ cups oat flakes
- ⅔ cup pumpkin seeds
- ½ cup flax seeds
- ½ cup pecans, chopped
- 3 Tbsp poppy seeds
- 2 Tbsp honey
- 1½–2 oz coconut oil
- 1½ cups water
- Salt to taste

DIRECTIONS

1. Combine all dry ingredients and mix well.
2. Add water and honey to the coconut oil and mix until combined and the honey is dissolved.
3. Combine dry and wet mixture and let the dough stand for 2 hours.
4. The dough must be soft and easy to knead. Add more water if needed.
5. Form the dough into a loaf and place it into a greased oven-proof pan, and bake at 356°F for 20 minutes.
6. Line a baking sheet with parchment paper. Remove the loaf from the oven and transfer it to the baking sheet and bake for 30 minutes more.

CINNABONS

SERVINGS: 3 | PREP TIME: 15 min. | COOK TIME: 15 min.

CARBS: 1.6 g | FAT: 7.1 g | PROTEIN: 7.4 g | CALORIES: 106

INGREDIENTS

- 2 eggs
- 6–7 oz cottage cheese
- ¼ tsp stevia
- ⅓ tsp baking powder
- ½ cup coconut flour

For filling:

- 2 tsp cinnamon
- ¼ tsp stevia
- 1 oz erythritol
- 2 Tbsp butter, melted

DIRECTIONS

1. Using a blender combine the cottage cheese, eggs, stevia and erythritol.
2. Add the coconut flour and baking powder and pulse to blend. (Add more flour if needed, depending on cottage cheese moisture content)
3. Cover the dough with plastic wrap and using a rolling pin roll out ¼ inch layer.
4. Brush melted butter over the layer.
5. Sprinkle all over with cinnamon.
6. Roll up the sheet of dough and cut into 8 pieces.
7. Line a baking sheet with parchment paper and place the cinnabon rolls on it.
8. Bake for 15 minutes at 356°F.

UNFLAVORED MUFFINS

SERVINGS: 1 | PREP TIME: 3 min. | COOK TIME: 12 min.

CARBS: 5 g | FAT: 6 g | PROTEIN: 7 g | CALORIES: 113

INGREDIENTS

- *1 egg*
- *2 tsp coconut flour*
- *¼ tsp baking powder*
- *Salt to taste*

DIRECTIONS

1. Whisk all ingredients to combine.
2. Grease muffin cups and pour in the dough.
3. Bake at 400°F for 12 minutes.

LEMON POPPYSEED MUFFINS

SERVINGS: 12 | PREP TIME: 5 min. | COOK TIME: 20 min.

CARBS: 3.3 g | FAT: 11.6 g | PROTEIN: 4 g | CALORIES: 99.8

INGREDIENTS

- 3 eggs
- ¼ cup butter, melted
- ¼ cup heavy cream
- 1 cup almond flour
- ⅓ cup erythritol
- 1 tsp baking powder
- 2 lemons, grated zest, juice (3 Tbsp)
- 2 Tbsp poppy seeds
- 25 drops liquid stevia

DIRECTIONS

1. Combine flour, erythritol and poppy seeds.
2. Stir in the melted butter, eggs, and heavy cream until smooth.
3. Add liquid stevia, lemon zest, lemon juice and baking powder.
4. Pour the dough into silicone molds or any muffin cups.
5. Bake at 350°F for 20 minutes.

LEMON COCONUT MUFFINS

SERVINGS: 16 | PREP TIME: 5 min. | COOK TIME: 20 min.

CARBS: 2 g | FAT: 7 g | PROTEIN: 3 g | CALORIES: 78

INGREDIENTS

- 3 eggs
- ¼ cup coconut flour
- 3 Tbsp coconut milk
- ½ cup coconut flakes
- ¼ cup butter
- ¼ cup erythritol
- Juice and grated zest of 1 lemon
- ½ tsp baking powder
- ½ tsp vanilla extract

DIRECTIONS

1. Whisk together butter and erythritol until smooth.
2. Mix in the eggs one at a time.
3. Add the vanilla extract, lemon juice, lemon zest and coconut milk, and beat until smooth.
4. Then add the flour, coconut flakes and baking powder.
5. Spoon the dough into greased muffin tins and bake at 400°F for 20 minutes.

APPLE ALMOND MUFFINS

SERVINGS: 12 | PREP TIME: 5 min. | COOK TIME: 15 min.

CARBS: 10 g | FAT: 15 g | PROTEIN: 5 g | CALORIES: 184

INGREDIENTS

- *2 eggs*
- *2 ½ cups almond flour*
- *⅓ cup butter, melted*
- *4 Tbsp honey*
- *1 tsp cinnamon*
- *1 apple, peeled, sliced thinly*

DIRECTIONS

1. Combine all ingredients except apple and give a good stir.
2. Stir in the apple slices.
3. Pour the dough into muffin cups and bake at 350°F for 15 minutes.

PUMPKIN MUFFINS

SERVINGS: 8 | PREP TIME: 15 min. | COOK TIME: 30 min.

CARBS: 16 g | FAT: 6 g | PROTEIN: 6 g | CALORIES: 137

INGREDIENTS

- *2 cups pumpkin seeds, ground*
- *4 eggs, separated*
- *¾ cup coconut sugar*
- *Dash of cinnamon*
- *1 tsp baking powder*

DIRECTIONS

1. Whip the egg whites with ½ cup coconut sugar until foamy.
2. Stir the egg yolks with ¼ cup coconut sugar.
3. Combine all dry ingredients — the pumpkin seed meal, baking powder and cinnamon.
4. Stir the egg yolks mixture into the flour mixture.
5. Gradually add egg whites mixture.
6. Pour the dough into a greased baking pan or muffin cups, and bake at 356°F for about 30 minutes.

DATE MUFFINS

SERVINGS: 8 | PREP TIME: 15 min. | COOK TIME: 40 min.

CARBS: 38 g | FAT: 8.4 g | PROTEIN: 3.6 g | CALORIES: 232

INGREDIENTS

- *8 oz dates, pitted, presoaked in 1 cup water for 1 hour, and then puréed in a blender*
- *2 eggs*
- *¼ cup coconut oil*
- *2 Tbsp maple syrup*
- *2 Tbsp coconut sugar*
- *1 cup coconut flour*
- *½ tsp baking powder*
- *½ tsp cinnamon*

DIRECTIONS

1. Blend the coconut oil with 2 Tbsp coconut sugar.
2. Constantly whisking, add in eggs, one at a time.
3. Add the date purée and 2 tablespoons maple syrup into the egg-oil mixture.
4. Combine baking powder with the flour and gradually add to the dates mixture. Blend well.
5. Pour into a baking pan lined with parchment paper or muffin cups and bake at 350°F for about 40 minutes.

MUFFINS WITH CRANBERRIES

SERVINGS: 12 | PREP TIME: 20 min. | COOK TIME: 20 min.

CARBS: 8 g | FAT: 0.8 g | PROTEIN: 5.4 g | CALORIES: 50

INGREDIENTS

- *2 Tbsp oat bran, ground*
- *1 Tbsp wheat bran, ground*
- *4 Tbsp powdered skim milk*
- *2 Tbsp cocoa powder*
- *4 eggs, separated*
- *1 tsp baking powder*
- *2 Tbsp cottage cheese*
- *Sweetener to taste*
- *2 Tbsp cranberries*
- *Dash of salt*

DIRECTIONS

1. Add all ingredients to egg yolks and knead the dough.
2. Add cranberries and mix carefully not to smash the berries. Let stand.
3. Whisk egg whites with dash of salt until foamy.
4. Add egg whites to the dough.
5. Spoon the dough into greased muffin cups and bake at 356°F for 15–20 min.

VEGETABLE MUFFINS

SERVINGS: 8 | PREP TIME: 15 min. | COOK TIME: 20 min.

CARBS: 2.1 g | FAT: 2.4 g | PROTEIN: 4.4 g | CALORIES: 48

INGREDIENTS

- ½ cup grated carrots
- ½ cup bell pepper, cubed
- ½ cup green peas
- 5 eggs
- ½ cup cheese, grated
- Salt and pepper to taste

DIRECTIONS

1. Mix vegetables in a salad bowl and season with salt and pepper.
2. Grease muffin cups and add the vegetable mixture filling about ⅔ of the cup.
3. Whisk eggs and add 2–3 Tbsp of the eggs to the cups.
4. Sprinkle with cheese about 1 tsp in each cup.
5. Bake at 374°F for 15–20 min.

BASIL BUNS

SERVINGS: 8 | PREP TIME: 15 min. | COOK TIME: 20 min.

CARBS: 1.4 g | FAT: 15 g | PROTEIN: 9.6 g | CALORIES: 186

INGREDIENTS

- *4 eggs*
- *¾ cup almond flour*
- *6 Tbsp butter*
- *6 garlic cloves, crushed*
- *5½ oz Parmesan, grated*
- *¾ cup water*
- *1 cup fresh basil, chopped*
- *Salt to taste*

DIRECTIONS

1. Heat water until boiling and add butter and salt. Add flour and mix until smooth. Remove from the hear.
2. Crack eggs into the dough one at a time, mixing after each egg. Add basil, garlic and, last, the Parmesan. Mix until smooth.
3. Line a baking sheet with parchment paper and place the dough on it one spoonful at a time to form buns.
4. Bake at 392°F for 20 minutes.

BARBEQUE BUNS

SERVINGS: 8 | PREP TIME: 15 min. | COOK TIME: 50 min.

CARBS: 12.1 g | FAT: 4.2 g | PROTEIN: 3.3 g | CALORIES: 91

INGREDIENTS

- *3 egg whites*
- *1 cup sunflower seeds, ground*
- *¼ cup flax meal*
- *5 Tbsp psyllium husks*
- *1 cup water, boiling*
- *2 tsp baking powder*
- *Salt to taste*

DIRECTIONS

1. Combine all dry ingredients. Add egg whites and, using a blender, whisk until smooth.
2. Add boiling water and keep whisking.
3. Line a baking sheet with parchment paper and drop the dough on it one spoonful at a time to form buns.
4. Bake at 356°F for 50 minutes.

SPRING ONION BUNS

SERVINGS: 6 | PREP TIME: 15 min. | COOK TIME: 30 min.

CARBS: 1.1 g | FAT: 6.7 g | PROTEIN: 4.2 g | CALORIES: 81

INGREDIENTS

- *3 eggs, separated*
- *3½ oz cream cheese*
- *1 tsp stevia*
- *½ tsp baking powder*
- *Salt to taste*

For filling:

- *1 egg, hard boiled, chopped*
- *2 sprigs spring onions, chopped*

DIRECTIONS

1. Combine egg yolks with stevia, cream cheese, baking powder and salt.
2. Whisk egg whites until foamy.
3. Using a spatula mix the egg whites into the yolk mixture.
4. Pour the dough into greased muffin cups filling ½ of the cup.
5. Combine spring onions with chopped egg and add this filling to muffin cups.
6. Pour more dough into the cups
7. Bake at 300°F for 30 minutes.

SQUASH MUFFINS

SERVINGS: 6 | PREP TIME: 10 min. | COOK TIME: 25 min.

CARBS: 3.4 g | FAT: 7.8 g | PROTEIN: 7.3 g | CALORIES: 111

INGREDIENTS

- *1 squash, peeled, grated*
- *2–3 spring onions, chopped*
- *1 Tbsp olive oil*
- *1 egg*
- *¼ cup plain yogurt*
- *1 cup almond flour*
- *½ cup hard cheese, grated*
- *⅔ tsp baking powder*
- *Salt to taste*

DIRECTIONS

1. Combine flour with salt and baking powder.
2. Whisk an egg and add olive oil to it as well as yogurt and half of the grated cheese. Give a good stir.
3. Combine the two mixtures.
4. Season the grated squash with salt and add to dough along with any accumulated liquid.
5. Add chopped spring onions to the dough.
6. Pour the dough into greased muffin cups ½ full and sprinkle with grated cheese.
7. Bake at 356°F for 25 minutes.

SESAME BUNS

SERVINGS: 12 | PREP TIME: 10 min. | COOK TIME: 50 min.

CARBS: 4 g | FAT: 6.5 g | PROTEIN: 6.9 g | CALORIES: 133

INGREDIENTS

- 6 egg whites
- 1 cup coconut flour
- 1 tsp baking powder
- 1 cup sesame seeds, separated (1/2 cup for the dough, ½ cup for coating)
- ½ cup pumpkin seeds
- ½ cup psyllium powder
- 1 cup water, hot
- Salt to taste

DIRECTIONS

1. Combine all dry ingredients except ½ cup of sesame seeds.
2. Whisk the egg whites until foamy.
3. Add foamy whites to dry ingredients, give a good stir.
4. Add 1 cup boiling water slowly, constantly stirring.
5. Put the remaining ½ cup sesame seeds in a separate bowl. With your hands shape round buns and coat in sesame seeds.
6. Line a baking sheet with parchment paper and place the buns on it.
7. Bake at 350°F for 50 minutes.

FLUFFY BUNS

SERVINGS: 10 | PREP TIME: 10 min. | COOK TIME: 50 min.

CARBS: 10 g | FAT: 3.5 g | PROTEIN: 6.7 g | CALORIES: 105

INGREDIENTS

- *2 eggs*
- *6 egg whites*
- *1½ cups almond flour*
- *½ cup coconut flour*
- *½ cup flax meal*
- *⅓ cup psyllium husk powder*
- *2 tsp cream of tartar*
- *2 tsp garlic powder*
- *2 tsp onion powder*
- *1 tsp baking soda*
- *Salt to taste*
- *2 cups water, boiling*
- *Seeds of your choice for sprinkling*

DIRECTIONS

1. Combine all dry ingredients.
2. Add the egg whites and whole eggs and mix well.
3. Add boiling water and mix until well combined.
4. Line a baking sheet with parchment paper and place the dough on it by spoonfuls leaving space between buns.
5. Sprinkle with seeds of your choice.
6. Bake at 350°F for 50 minutes.

MOZZARELLA BAGELS

SERVINGS: 6 | PREP TIME: 30 min. | COOK TIME: 15 min.

CARBS: 6 g | FAT: 21 g | PROTEIN: 12 g | CALORIES: 245

INGREDIENTS

- *1 egg*
- *1½ cups almond flour*
- *1½ cup mozzarella, shredded*
- *2 oz cream cheese, cut into pieces*
- *1 tsp baking powder*
- *1 Tbsp oat fiber*

DIRECTIONS

1. Microwave mozzarella and cream cheese for 1 minute. Stir and microwave for 30 seconds more.
2. In a food processor combine egg with microwaved cheese.
3. Add dry ingredients and process well.
4. Scrape the dough out, wrap in plastic wrap, and place in the freezer for 20 minutes.
5. Preheat oven to 400°F and line a baking sheet with parchment paper.
6. Divide the dough into 6 portions.
7. Roll each piece into a sausage shape and seal the ends together forming a ring.
8. Place on the parchment paper and bake for 12–15 minutes.

PROTEIN BUNS

SERVINGS: 8 | PREP TIME: 10 min. | COOK TIME: 40 min.

CARBS: 0.1 g | FAT: 0.3 g | PROTEIN: 6.4 g | CALORIES: 29

INGREDIENTS

- *2 eggs*
- *½ cup water*
- *1½–2 oz soya protein powder*
- *Stevia to taste (1 dash)*
- *Cinnamon or vanilla extract to taste*

DIRECTIONS

1. Whisk eggs, and then add other ingredients and whisk well.
2. Divide between 8 greased silicone cups and bake at 430°F for 20 minutes.
3. Lower the temperature to 340°F and bake for 10–15 minutes more.

BUNS WITH COTTAGE CHEESE

SERVINGS: 8 | PREP TIME: 10 min. | COOK TIME: 15 min.

CARBS: 6.7 g | FAT: 5.2 g | PROTEIN: 5.8 g | CALORIES: 77

INGREDIENTS

- *2 eggs*
- *3 oz almond flour or almond meal*
- *1 oz erythritol*
- *⅛ tsp stevia*
- *Cinnamon and vanilla extract to taste*

DIRECTIONS

1. Prepare the filling by mixing its ingredients; cottage cheese with egg, cinnamon and vanilla
2. Combine eggs with almond flour or meal, blend until smooth. Add erythritol, stevia and flavors to taste.
3. Spoon about 1 Tbsp dough into silicone cups. Spoon about 1 tsp filling on top ,and bake at 356°F for 15 minutes.

SANDWICH BUNS

SERVINGS: 6-8 | PREP TIME: 10 min. | COOK TIME: 25 min.

CARBS: 10 g | FAT: 6 g | PROTEIN: 5.3 g | CALORIES: 99

INGREDIENTS

- 4 eggs
- 2½ oz almond flour
- 1 Tbsp coconut flour
- 1 oz psyllium
- 1½ cups eggplant, finely grated, juices drained
- 3 Tbsp sesame seeds
- 1½ tsp baking powder
- Salt to taste

DIRECTIONS

1. Whisk eggs until foamy, and then add grated eggplant.
2. In a separate bowl mix all dry ingredients.
3. Add them to the egg mixture. Mix well.
4. Line a baking sheet with parchment paper and shape the buns with your hands.
5. Bake at 374°F for 20–25 min.

FLAX BUNS

SERVINGS: 6 | PREP TIME: 10 min. | COOK TIME: 20 min.

CARBS: 7 g | FAT: 5 g | PROTEIN: 5.9 g | CALORIES: 85

INGREDIENTS

- *1 egg*
- *2 egg whites*
- *1¾ oz flax seeds*
- *1¾ oz (about ½ cup) oat bran, ground*
- *1¾ oz buttermilk*
- *1 tsp baking powder*
- *Salt to taste*

DIRECTIONS

1. Combine dry ingredients. Add 1 egg and 2 egg whites, whisk well. Add buttermilk, whisk.
2. Spoon the dough into muffin cups and bake at 356°F for 20 minutes.

EGGPLANT MUFFFINS

SERVINGS: 3 | PREP TIME: 15 min. | COOK TIME: 20 min.

CARBS: 5.7 g | FAT: 14.2 g | PROTEIN: 8 g | CALORIES: 194

INGREDIENTS

- *2 eggplants, peeled and cubed*
- *¾ cup mozzarella*
- *2 Tbsp butter, melted*
- *1 Tbsp fresh basil, chopped*
- *1 tsp garlic powder*
- *½ tsp dried basil*

DIRECTIONS

1. Preheat the oven to 374°F.
2. Mix garlic powder and dried basil, and add melted butter.
3. Place the cubed eggplant on the bottom of 3 baking cups.
4. Sprinkle with mozzarella and 1 tsp melted butter mixture.
5. Layer the eggplants again, then cheese, then butter. Sprinkle with the remaining cheese.
6. Bake for 20 minutes until golden.

KETO PIZZA

SERVINGS: 1 | PREP TIME: 10 min. | COOK TIME: 20 min.

CARBS: 3.5 g | FAT: 35 g | PROTEIN: 27 g | CALORIES: 459

INGREDIENTS

- *2 eggs*
- *2 tablespoons parmesan cheese*
- *1 tablespoon psyllium husk powder*
- *½ tsp Italian seasoning*
- *Salt*
- *2 teaspoons frying oil*
- *1 ½ ounces mozzarella cheese*
- *3 tablespoon tomato sauce*
- *1 tablespoon chopped basil*

DIRECTIONS

1. Place the parmesan, psyllium husk powder, Italian seasoning and salt into a blender with two eggs and blend.
2. Heat a large frying pan and add the oil.
3. Add the mixture to the pan in a large circular shape.
4. Flip once the underside is browning and then remove from pan.
5. Spoon the tomato sauce onto the pizza crust and spread.
6. Add the cheese and spread over the top of the pizza.
7. Place the pizza into the oven – it is finished once the cheese is melted.

PIZZA FRITTATA

SERVINGS: 8 | PREP TIME: 15 min. | COOK TIME: 30 min.

CARBS: 2.1 g | FAT: 23.8 g | PROTEIN: 19.4 g | CALORIES: 298

INGREDIENTS

- 12 eggs
- 9 ounce bag frozen spinach
- 1 ounce pepperoni
- 5 ounces mozzarella cheese
- 1 teaspoon garlic, minced
- ½ cup ricotta cheese
- ½ cup parmesan cheese,
- 4 tablespoon olive oil
- ¼ teaspoon nutmeg
- Salt
- Pepper

DIRECTIONS

1. Microwave the spinach on defrost.
2. Preheat your oven to 375°F.
3. Combine the ricotta, the parmesan and spinach.
4. Pour the mixture into a baking dish.
5. Sprinkle the mozzarella over the mixture.
6. Add the pepperoni.
7. Bake for half an hour, until set.

OATMEAL COOKIES

SERVINGS: 15 | PREP TIME: 10 min. | COOK TIME: 20 min.

CARBS: 8.6 g | FAT: 0.9 g | PROTEIN: 2.5 g | CALORIES: 51

INGREDIENTS

- *3 eggs*
- *2 cups oat flakes, ground*
- *⅓ tsp vanilla extract*
- *Dash of cinnamon*
- *2 tsp erythritol*

DIRECTIONS

1. Whisk eggs and add vanilla extract.
2. In a separate bowl combine oatmeal, erythritol and cinnamon. Add the egg mixture and combine
3. Line a baking sheet with parchment paper and put the cookie batter on it by spoonfuls.
4. Bake at 392°F for 15–20 minutes.

OATMEAL BANANA COOKIES

SERVINGS: 10 | PREP TIME: 20 min. | COOK TIME: 30 min.

CARBS: 6 g | FAT: 1.2 g | PROTEIN: 5.2 g | CALORIES: 120

INGREDIENTS

- *8 oz cottage cheese, fat free*
- *1 cup oatmeal*
- *1 apple, peeled, cored, grated*
- *1 banana*
- *1 Tbsp lemon juice*
- *1 tsp honey*

DIRECTIONS

1. Mix the cottage cheese with the honey and oatmeal.
2. Combine grated apple with lemon juice. Mash the banana with a fork.
3. Mix all ingredients together.
4. Line a baking sheet with parchment paper and spoon the cookies onto it.
5. Bake at 392°F for 30 minutes.

OAT STICKS

SERVINGS: 10 | PREP TIME: 15 min. | COOK TIME: 12 min.

CARBS: 7.5 g | FAT: 10.2 g | PROTEIN: 4 g | CALORIES: 137

INGREDIENTS

- *1 cup oat flakes, finely ground*
- *2½ oz butter, cubed*
- *2 oz cheese of your choice, grated*
- *1 cup milk*
- *½ cup almond flour*
- *Salt to taste*

DIRECTIONS

1. Combine oat flakes, flour and salt.
2. Add butter, milk and grated cheese and mix thoroughly.
3. Knead the dough. It will be thick.
4. Roll out the dough about ¼inch thick with a rolling pin, and cut into sticks.
5. Line a baking sheet with parchment paper and place the sticks on it.
6. Bake at 380° F for 12 minutes.

SIMPLE COOKIES

SERVINGS: 10 | PREP TIME: 15 min. | COOK TIME: 20 min.

CARBS: 7.5 g | FAT: 10.2 g | PROTEIN: 4 g | CALORIES: 137

INGREDIENTS

- *2 cups flakes of your choice (oat/buckwheat/mix)*
- *1 egg*
- *2 cups water*
- *Sweetener of your choice to taste*

DIRECTIONS

1. Dissolve the sweetener in water and add the flakes. Let soak for 10 minutes. Add more water if needed.
2. Add an egg and mix well.
3. Line a baking sheet with parchment paper and, shaping by hand, place the cookies on the paper.
4. Bake at 380° F for 20 minutes.

PUMPKIN ALMOND COOKIES

SERVINGS: 12 | PREP TIME: 20 min. | COOK TIME: 30 min.

CARBS: 26 g | FAT: 20 g | PROTEIN: 8.3 g | CALORIES: 315

INGREDIENTS

- *1 egg white*
- *1 cup pumpkin purée*
- *1 cup almond flour*
- *1 cup almonds, ground*
- *2 Tbsp maple syrup*
- *¼ cup coconut flakes*
- *¼ cup lemon zest, grated*

DIRECTIONS

1. Combine flour, almonds, coconut flakes and lemon zest.
2. In a separate bowl whisk egg white until foamy. Gradually add maple syrup.
3. Mix all ingredients together with pumpkin purée.
4. Line a baking sheet with parchment paper and add the cookies by the spoonful.
5. Bake at 302°F for 30 minutes.

COCONUT COOKIES

SERVINGS: 12 | PREP TIME: 10 min. | COOK TIME: 7 min.

CARBS: 30 g | FAT: 10.4 g | PROTEIN: 1.4 g | CALORIES: 144

INGREDIENTS

- *2 egg whites*
- *1½ cups coconut flakes*
- *½ stick (2 oz) butter, melted, cooled*
- *2 Tbsp coconut flour*
- *1 cup erythritol*

DIRECTIONS

1. Combine flour, coconut flakes and erythritol.
2. Add egg whites and melted butter. Give a good stir.
3. Line a baking sheet with parchment paper and put the cookie batter on it by the spoonfuls.
4. Bake at 392°F for 7 minutes.

COCONUT BALLS

SERVINGS: 12 | PREP TIME: 10 min. | COOK TIME: 15 min.

CARBS: 6 g | FAT: 55 g | PROTEIN: 20.3 g | CALORIES: 144

INGREDIENTS

- *3 egg whites*
- *1 Tbsp coconut flour*
- *2½ oz coconut flakes*
- *Sweetener of your choice to taste*

DIRECTIONS

1. Whisk egg whites until foamy.
2. Combine flour with coconut flakes and add to egg foam. Mix with a spoon, not a blender.
3. Shape into balls and place on a baking sheet lined with parchment paper.
4. Bake at 392°F for 15 minutes.

APPLE CARROT COOKIES

SERVINGS: 10 | PREP TIME: 10 min. | COOK TIME: 30 min.

CARBS: 5.4 g | FAT: 0.6 g | PROTEIN: 0.9 g | CALORIES: 29

INGREDIENTS

- *1 apple, peeled, grated*
- *1 carrot, grated*
- *1 egg white*
- *4 Tbsp oatmeal*
- *½ tsp cinnamon*
- *Handful of raisins*
- *1 tsp stevia*

DIRECTIONS

1. Combine all ingredients and give a good stir.
2. Line a baking sheet with parchment paper and spoon the cookies onto it.
3. Bake at 392°F for 20–30 minutes.

CREAM CHEESE COOKIES

SERVINGS: 24 | PREP TIME: 10 min. | COOK TIME: 15 min.

CARBS: 3 g | FAT: 9 g | PROTEIN: 3 g | CALORIES: 106

INGREDIENTS

- *1 egg white*
- *¼ cup butter, soft*
- *3 cups almond flour*
- *2 oz cream cheese*
- *2 tsp vanilla extract*
- *¾ cup erythritol*

DIRECTIONS

1. Beat together the butter, cream cheese, and erythritol.
2. Add vanilla and egg white.
3. Gradually sift flour, ½ cup at a time into the mixture.
4. Line a baking sheet with parchment paper and spoon the cookies onto it.
5. Bake at 350°F for 15 minutes.

CRISPY COOKIES

SERVINGS: 12 | PREP TIME: 5 min. | COOK TIME: 15 min.

CARBS: 11 g | FAT: 2.1 g | PROTEIN: 12.3 g | CALORIES: 104

INGREDIENTS

- *2 eggs*
- *1 Tbsp soy flour*
- *3 Tbsp oat bran*
- *1–2 tsp coconut chips*
- *½ cup milk*
- *Dash of baking soda*
- *Vanilla extract to taste*
- *Sweetener of your choice to taste*

DIRECTIONS

1. Combine all ingredients and let stand for 15 minutes. The dough will be watery but this is OK.
2. Pour the dough into silicone molds, about 1 Tbsp into each.
3. Bake at 390°F for 15–20 minutes.

CRACKERS WITH FLAX SEEDS

SERVINGS: 10 | PREP TIME: 20 min. | COOK TIME: 20 min.

CARBS: 10.8 g | FAT: 5.9 g | PROTEIN: 3 g | CALORIES: 104

INGREDIENTS

- *2 Tbsp flax seeds*
- *⅓ cup milk*
- *2 Tbsp coconut oil*
- *1 cup coconut flour*
- *½ tsp baking powder*
- *1 tsp erythritol*

DIRECTIONS

1. Combine flour with baking powder, erythritol and flax seeds.
2. Gradually add milk and oil and knead the dough.
3. Wrap the dough in plastic wrap and put in the fridge for 15 minutes.
4. Divide the dough into 2 parts and roll it out with a rolling pin about 0.1 inch thick.
5. Cut out triangles.
6. Line a baking sheet with parchment paper and place the crackers on it.
7. Bake at 390°F for 20 minutes.

RYE CRACKERS

SERVINGS: 10 | PREP TIME: 10 min. | COOK TIME: 15 min.

CARBS: 10.4 g | FAT: 4.3 g | PROTEIN: 1.1 g | CALORIES: 80

INGREDIENTS

- *1 cup rye flour*
- *⅔ cup bran*
- *2 tsp baking powder*
- *3 Tbsp vegetable oil*
- *1 tsp liquid malt extract*
- *1 tsp apple vinegar*
- *1 cup water*
- *Salt to taste*

DIRECTIONS

1. Combine flour with bran, baking powder and salt.
2. Pour in oil, vinegar and malt extract. Mix well.
3. Knead the dough, gradually adding the water.
4. Divide the dough into 2 parts and roll it out with a rolling pin about 0.1 inch thick.
5. Cut out (using a knife or cookie cutter) the crackers of square or rectangle shape.
6. Line a baking sheet with parchment paper and place the crackers on it
7. Bake at 390°F for 12–15 minutes.

GOAT CHEESE CRACKERS

SERVINGS: 12 | PREP TIME: 5 min. | COOK TIME: 15 min.

CARBS: 2 g | FAT: 8 g | PROTEIN: 4 g | CALORIES: 99

INGREDIENTS

- 6 oz goat cheese
- ½ cup coconut flour
- 4 Tbsp butter
- 2 Tbsp fresh rosemary
- 1 tsp baking powder

DIRECTIONS

1. In a food processor combine all ingredients and process until smooth.
2. Roll out the dough with a rolling pin to about ¼–½ inch thick and cut out the crackers with a knife or cookie cutter.
3. Line a baking sheet with parchment paper and place the crackers on it.
4. Bake at 380°F for 15–20 minutes.

DRIED FRUIT COOKIES

SERVINGS: 10 | PREP TIME: 10 min. | COOK TIME: 15 min.

CARBS: 33 g | FAT: 20.3 g | PROTEIN: 6.4 g | CALORIES: 340

INGREDIENTS

- *2 cups oat flakes, toasted with butter in a frying pan*
- *1 stick butter (4 oz)*
- *1 egg*
- *1 cup milk*
- *2 Tbsp coconut chips*
- *2 0z almonds, ground*
- *2 oz hazelnuts, ground*
- *1¾ 0z prunes, chopped*
- *1 tsp cinnamon*
- *4 Tbsp erythritol*

DIRECTIONS

1. Combine oats, nuts, prunes, cinnamon and erythritol
2. Add milk and coconut, mix well.
3. Add the egg and give a good stir.
4. Shape the batter into cookies. Line a baking sheet with parchment paper and place the cookies on it.
5. Bake at 390°F for 15 minutes.

GINGER COOKIES

SERVINGS: 10 | PREP TIME: 10 min. | COOK TIME: 15 min.

CARBS: 2.4 g | FAT: 1.1 g | PROTEIN: 1.6 g | CALORIES: 21

INGREDIENTS

- *3 Tbsp oat bran*
- *2 egg whites*
- *1 Tbsp dried ginger*
- *1 tsp plain cow's milk yogurt*
- *1 tsp baking powder*
- *Sweetener of your choice to taste*

DIRECTIONS

1. Combine all ingredients. Add more bran if the dough is too runny. Mix well.
2. Line a baking sheet with parchment paper and spoon the cookies onto it
3. Bake at 356°F for 15 minutes.

CHOCOLATE CHIP COOKIES

SERVINGS: 15 | PREP TIME: 10 min. | COOK TIME: 15 min.

CARBS: 5 g | FAT: 16 g | PROTEIN: 4 g | CALORIES: 195

INGREDIENTS

- 1 cup coconut flour
- ½ cup butter, soft
- 1 cup unsweetened coconut flakes
- 4 eggs
- 2⅔ oz dark chocolate chips
- ½ tsp vanilla extract
- ½ cup erythritol

DIRECTIONS

1. Mix the butter, erythritol, vanilla, eggs and salt together.
2. Add the coconut flour, coconut flakes and chocolate chips. Stir and mix well.
3. Line a baking sheet with parchment paper and spoon the cookies onto it.
4. Bake at 375°F for 15–20 minutes.

JAPANESE COOKIES

SERVINGS: 8 | PREP TIME: 10 min. | COOK TIME: 10 min.

CARBS: 10 g | FAT: 1.6 g | PROTEIN: 3.6 g | CALORIES: 46

INGREDIENTS

- *1 egg yolk*
- *2 Tbsp powdered milk + 1 tsp cow's milk*
- *1 Tbsp cocoa powder*
- *2 Tbsp erythritol*
- *1 Tbsp starch*

DIRECTIONS

1. Whisk egg yolk with erythritol until well combined.
2. Add starch, powdered milk, cocoa powder and milk. Knead the dough and shape it into a ball.
3. With your hands roll the ball out to form a long " snake" Cut it and form small balls
4. Line a baking sheet with parchment paper .Form the small balls into cookies and place them on the paper.
5. Bake at 320° F for 10 minutes.
6. Use chopped peanuts instead of cocoa powder for white Japanese cookies.

CONCLUSION

Thank you for reading this book and having the patience to try the recipes.

I do hope that you have had as much enjoyment reading and experimenting with the meals as I have had writing the book.

Stay safe and healthy!

RECIPE INDEX

Dry Weights

oz	(spoon)	C	(scale)	(scale)
1/2 OZ	1 Tbsp	1/16 C	15 g	
1 OZ	2 Tbsp	1/8 C	28 g	
2 OZ	4 Tbsp	1/4 C	57 g	
3 OZ	6 Tbsp	1/3 C	85 g	
4 OZ	8 Tbsp	1/2 C	115 g	1/4 lb
8 OZ	16 Tbsp	1 C	227 g	1/2 lb
12 OZ	24 Tbsp	1 1/2 C	340 g	3/4 lb
16 OZ	32 Tbsp	2 C	455 g	1 lb

Liquid Conversions

1 Gallon:
4 quarts
8 pints
16 cups
128 fl oz
3.8 liters

1 Quart:
2 pints
4 cups
32 fl oz
0.95 liters

1 Pint:
2 cups
16 fl oz
480 ml

1 Cup:
16 Tbsp
8 fl oz
240 ml

---

oz	(spoon)	(spoon)	mL	C	Pt	Qt
1 oz	6 tsp	2 Tbsp	30 ml	1/8 C		
2 oz	12 tsp	4 Tbsp	60 ml	1/4 C		
2 2/3 oz	16 tsp	5 Tbsp	80 ml	1/3 C		
4 oz	24 tsp	8 Tbsp	120 ml	1/2 C		
5 1/3 oz	32 tsp	11 Tbsp	160 ml	2/3 C		
6 oz	36 tsp	12 Tbsp	177 ml	3/4 C		
8 oz	48 tsp	16 Tbsp	237 ml	1 C	1/2 pt	1/4 qt
16 oz	96 tsp	32 Tbsp	480 ml	2 C	1 pt	1/2 qt
32 oz	192 tsp	64 Tbsp	950 ml	4 C	2 pt	1 qt

Fahrenheit to Celcius (F to C)

500 F = 260 C
475 F = 245 C
450 F = 235 C
425 F = 220 C
400 F = 205 C
375 F = 190 C
350 F = 180 C
325 F = 160 C
300 F = 150 C
275 F = 135 C
250 F = 120 C
225 F = 107 C

Safe Cooking Meat Temperatures

1 Tbsp: 15 ml

1 tsp: 5 ml

Minimum temperatures:

USDA Safe at 145 F	USDA Safe at 160 F	USDA Safe at 165 F
Beef Steaks, Briskets, and Roasts; Pork Chops, Roasts, Ribs, Shoulders, and Butts; Lamb Chops, Legs, and Roasts; Fresh Hams, Veal Steaks, Fish, and Shrimp	Ground Meats (except poultry)	Chicken & Turkey, ground or whole